BASOTHO

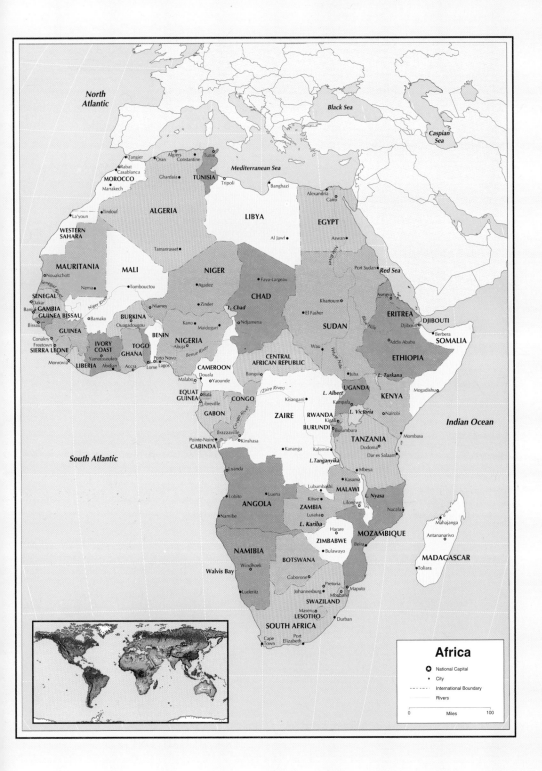

North
Atlantic

Black Sea

Caspian
Sea

Tangier
Algiers Tunis
Oran Constantine
Rabat
Casablanca MOROCCO
Marrakech Ghardaïa TUNISIA Tripoli
Mediterranean Sea
Banghazi

La'youn Tindouf ALGERIA LIBYA Alexandria Cairo

WESTERN
SAHARA EGYPT

Tamanrasset Al Jawf Aswan

MAURITANIA MALI NIGER Port Sudan Red Sea
Nouakchott
Senegal River Nema Tombouctou Agadez Faya-Largeau Asmera
SENEGAL CHAD Khartoum ERITREA
Dakar Zinder L. Chad SUDAN DJIBOUTI
Banjul GAMBIA Niamey El Fasher Djibouti
GUINEA BISSAU Niger River Bamako BURKINA Kano Ndjamena Blue Nile Berbera
Bissau GUINEA Ouagadougou Maiduguri SOMALIA
Conakry BENIN NIGERIA Wau Addis Ababa
Freetown TOGO Abuja Benue River White Nile ETHIOPIA
SIERRA LEONE IVORY GHANA CENTRAL Juba L. Turkana
Monrovia COAST Porto Novo AFRICAN REPUBLIC
LIBERIA Abidjan Accra Lome Lagos CAMEROON Bangui UGANDA Mogadishu
Yamoussoukro Douala L. Albert KENYA
EQUAT Bata Yaounde (Zaire River) Kisangani Kampala
GUINEA Libreville CONGO L. Victoria Nairobi
GABON ZAIRE RWANDA Indian Ocean
Brazzaville Kigali BURUNDI
Pointe-Noire Kinshasa Bujumbura TANZANIA Mombasa
CABINDA Kananga Dodoma
Kalemie Dar es Salaam

South Atlantic L.Tanganyika
Luanda Mbeya
Lobito Luena Lubumbashi Kasama
MALAWI L. Nyasa
ANGOLA Kitwe Lilongwe Nacala
Namibe ZAMBIA Lusaka
L. Kariba
NAMIBIA Harare MOZAMBIQUE
Walvis Bay ZIMBABWE Beira
Windhoek BOTSWANA Bulawayo MADAGASCAR
Mahajanga
Antananarivo
Toliara
Gaborone
Luderitz Johannesburg Pretoria Maputo
Mbabane
SWAZILAND Durban
Maseru
LESOTHO
SOUTH AFRICA
Cape Port
Town Elizabeth

The Heritage Library of African Peoples

BASOTHO

Gary N. van Wyk, Ph.D.

THE ROSEN PUBLISHING GROUP, INC.
NEW YORK

Published in 1996 by The Rosen Publishing Group, Inc.
29 East 21st Street, New York, NY 10010

Copyright 1996 by The Rosen Publishing Group, Inc.

First Edition

Manufactured in the United States of America

Library of Congress Cataloging-in-Publication Data

Van Wyk, Gary.
    Basotho / Gary van Wyk. — 1st ed.
      p. cm. — (The heritage library of African peoples)
    Includes bibliographical references and index.
    Summary: Surveys the history, culture, and contemporary life of the Basotho people of South Africa and Lesotho.
    ISBN 0-8239-2005-4
    1. Sotho (African people)—History—Juvenile literature. 2. Sotho (African people)—Social life and customs—Juvenile literature.
[1. Sotho (African people)] I. Title. II. Series.
DT1768.S68V36   1996
968'.004963977—dc20   96-16127
                                                            CIP
                                                                AC

Contents

INTRODUCTION

THERE IS EVERY REASON FOR US TO KNOW something about Africa and to understand its past and the way of life of its peoples. Africa is a rich continent that has for centuries provided the world with art, culture, labor, wealth, and natural resources. It has vast mineral deposits, fossil fuels, and commercial crops.

But perhaps most important is the fact that fossil evidence indicates that human beings originated in Africa. The earliest traces of human beings and their tools are almost two million years old. Their descendants have migrated throughout the world. To be human is to be of African descent.

The experiences of the peoples who stayed in Africa are as rich and as diverse as of those who established themselves elsewhere. This series of books describes their environment, their modes of subsistence, their relationships, and their customs and beliefs. The books present the variety of languages, histories, cultures, and religions that are to be found on the African continent. They demonstrate the historical linkages between African peoples and the way contemporary Africa has been affected by European colonial rule.

Africa is large, complex, and diverse. It encompasses an area of more than 11,700,000

square miles. The United States, Europe, and India could fit easily into it. The sheer size is an indication of the continent's great variety in geography, terrain, climate, flora, fauna, peoples, languages, and cultures.

Much of contemporary Africa has been shaped by European colonial rule, industrialization, urbanization, and the demands of a world economic system. For more than seventy years, large regions of Africa were ruled by Great Britain, France, Belgium, Portugal, and Spain. African peoples from various ethnic, linguistic, and cultural backgrounds were brought together to form colonial states.

For decades Africans struggled to gain their independence. It was not until after World War II that the colonial territories became independent African states. Today, almost all of Africa is ruled by Africans. Large numbers of Africans live in modern cities. Rural Africa is also being transformed, and yet its people still engage in many of their customs and beliefs.

Contemporary circumstances and natural events have not always been kind to ordinary Africans. Today, however, new popular social movements and technological innovations pose great promise for future development.

George C. Bond, Ph.D., Director
Institute of African Studies
Columbia University, New York

Basotho are noted for their rich artistic and ceremonial heritage. This diviner's beaded skirt echoes the floral designs on the house behind her. Flowers are Basotho symbols of fertility and beauty.

PREFACE

SOUTHERN AFRICA HAS BEEN TRANSFORMED by the dramatic arrival of democracy in South Africa, the last African country to emerge from colonial and cultural domination and minority rule. The world watched in wonder as the elections of 1994 peacefully concluded South Africa's long quest for freedom. South Africa's new constitution and bill of rights, arguably the most progressive in the world, are a high point in African and world history.

Now Southern African scholars are finally free to present their history, their rich heritage, and the heroic efforts their peoples have made to the region. There is a wide audience eager for these truths that have been distorted and silenced for so long. The timely Heritage Library of African Peoples series on Southern Africa can play an invaluable role in cementing people's appreciation of their own heritage; in fostering understanding among all the peoples of the region; and in sharing with readers worldwide the unique and fascinating cultures of Southern Africa.

As a Mosotho and a Southern African, I wholeheartedly welcome the insightful Basotho book and this Southern African series.

T. T. Thahane, Deputy Governor of the
South African Reserve Bank; former
Vice President of the World Bank (retired).

At their graduation ceremony, initiated Basotho women display relatives' gifts attached to reed mats that the women have made. The reeds, red ocher around their necks, and the dots in their hair that represent seeds all emphasize women's connection to earth and plants. Beauty and composure are also important aspects of the ceremony.

chapter

1

THE LAND AND THE PEOPLE

▼ BASOTHO ▼

The South Sotho people call themselves
Basotho (ba-soo-too) in their own language,
which is called Sesotho (sess-oo-too). "Lesotho"
(less-oo-too) means the land of Basotho, and it
is the name of their independent country.

The name "Basotho" means "the Sotho
people." Basotho are thus sometimes referred to
simply as "the Sotho." However, this can cause
confusion, because there are other related Sotho
peoples in Southern Africa. The other Sotho
peoples include Western Sotho or Batswana
groups, who speak Setswana, and various North
Sotho groups, who mostly speak Sepedi.

The various Sotho languages and traditions
are similar, but there are also many differences
in the history, culture, and present situation of
the different Sotho groups.

All these Sotho-speaking peoples are part of

the Bantu-speaking peoples who occupy most of sub-Saharan Africa. The ancestors of many early Basotho were a people called Bakoena (buk-when-uh). They settled north of Johannesburg and Pretoria around 1200AD in the Magaliesberg Mountains, which are named after the great Bakoena chief, Mohale. "Bakoena" means The People of the Crocodile, indicating that the crocodile is their totem animal—their group symbol, whose praises they sang, and which they would never kill or eat. The crocodile remains a national symbol in Lesotho.

By about 1500, some Bakoena had migrated south into the present-day Free State province of South Africa. By the 1600s, they had settled in the Caledon River valley. Among the people who preceded them into this area were the Tlokoa or Batlokoa (but-lok-wa), The People of the Wild Cat, who became enemies of Basotho.

This region's climate is pleasant. The land is fertile, grazing is lush, and in the past the hunting was good and there were plenty of wild foods to gather. Peoples in this area made metal tools, weapons, and ornaments and traded with people at the coast and in the interior. In the summer, when rainfall is highest, women grew grains, squashes, and beans. Men herded sheep, goats, and cattle year-round.

As is true in many Bantu societies, cattle were central to the people's lives. Wealth was stored

The national state of Basotho is Lesotho (above). Basotho in South Africa and Lesotho use slightly different spellings for place names and other words. For example, "Butha Buthe" is spelled "Botha-Bothe" by Basotho living in Lesotho. Areas where Basotho populations are concentrated are shaded on the map below.

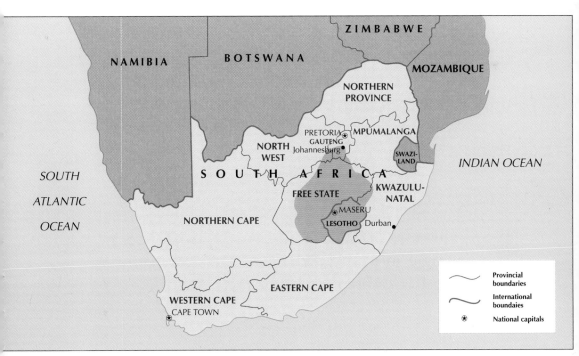

and measured in cattle. To marry and start a family, a man had to give the bride's family *bohali*, a number of cattle, in recognition of their efforts in raising her. Cattle were also an important link between humans and the spiritual world, because cattle were sacrificed to the ancestors on important occasions.

Boys spent much of their time herding animals. They knew all their cattle by name, and developed strong bonds with them. It was an honored tradition for young men from neighboring groups to carry out cattle raids on one another. This was also a quick way to acquire wealth.

An ambitious man who acquired many cattle could use them to marry several wives, thus building up a large family and networks of in-laws. He could also attract a loyal following by lending cattle to less fortunate people and in this way become a minor chief. This pattern encouraged widely scattered small communities under independent chiefs. Neighboring chiefs were rivals or allies, depending on their relationship.

▼ LESOTHO ▼

Today, many Basotho live in Lesotho. Formerly called Basutoland, it was controlled by Britain until 1966. Lesotho is the world's only landlocked country that is completely sur-

rounded by only one other country: South
Africa. Although surrounded by white settlers
and colonists in the 1800s, Lesotho kept control
over its own territory through outstanding
leadership by Moshoeshoe (maw-shweh-shweh),
the first Basotho king.

Britain and South Africa tried to incorporate
Lesotho into South Africa many times. To preserve its separation, Lesotho was forced to
surrender much land. Today, Lesotho is econom-
ically reliant on South Africa in many ways.
About half of Lesotho's adult male population
and many women are migrant workers in South
Africa and spend most of their time there. Their
earnings make up about two-thirds of Lesotho's
income. The population of Lesotho, estimated at
1.89 million in 1992, is thus largely outside the
country, working in South Africa.

Since the late 1800s, most male migrants
have taken jobs in the gold mines close to
Johannesburg. In some rural communities, working in the mines is seen as both a part of a
young man's education and a test of his tough-
ness. This is because it is hard and dangerous
work. The migrant labor system creates many
social problems. It splits up families and is very
hard on the women in Lesotho who must raise
children and run households on their own.

Excluding these Basotho migrants, whose
official home remains Lesotho, more Basotho

Lesotho is a poor and mountainous country (above). Most of its fertile land became part of South Africa's Free State province (below). Basotho thus live in widely different environments. The stone-walled cattle enclosures seen above are an ancient feature of Basotho settlements.

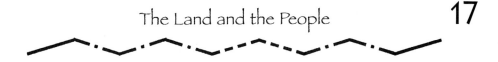

live permanently in South Africa than in Lesotho itself. Many live in South African cities. Many others are farmworkers living on white-owned farms in the Free State province of South Africa. About 70 percent of the Free State population is Basotho. The rich farming areas there once belonged to Basotho, but they were forced off them in the 1800s during a series of wars with Britain and the Afrikaner Boers.

▼ THE COLONIAL PERIOD ▼

The Boers were frontier settlers, mostly of Dutch background. They trekked into the interior of South Africa to escape Britain's authority over the Cape Colony based in Cape Town. Boers invaded Basotho land from 1835 onward, after slavery was abolished at the Cape. They refused to recognize black people as equals who should be paid for their work.

At first the Boers were guests of Moshoeshoe, who allowed them to graze their cattle and farm on Basotho lands. According to Basotho law, land is not privately owned. All land is held in trust by the chief. He lends it for use to those who accept his authority over it. The Boers accepted this system at first, but soon they began to claim ownership of the land that had been lent to them, and they wanted more.

Great tensions developed between Basotho

and the Boers. This worried Britain, because it added to the disturbances on the unstable frontiers of the Cape Colony. Every time there was a major dispute between Basotho and the Boers, Britain intervened on the side of the Boers. It often did so unfairly, because it had formal agreements with Moshoeshoe, who recognized British authority and cooperated with it while the rebellious Boers did not.

To calm the Boers during disputes, the British forced Basotho to surrender more and more of the fertile land of Lesotho that they needed to survive. By 1869, Basotho were left only with rugged mountains and the narrow strip of fertile land south of the Caledon River. This became the modern country of Lesotho.

▼ LIFE TODAY ▼

Today, Lesotho is small, poor, and very mountainous. It is the only country in the world that lies entirely 5,000 feet above sea level. In the winter it is very cold and often snow-covered. Lesotho's most important natural resource is water, which is exported to South Africa. Many of Southern Africa's major rivers have their sources in Lesotho's mountains. Water is stored in huge dams and sent to South Africa via gigantic irrigation tunnels that cut through the mountains.

There is no notable industry or manufacturing in Lesotho. Farming adds little wealth to the

Basotho herdboys wear brightly patterned blankets against the cold. These boys are playing *marabaraba*, a game like checkers. They have scratched into the rock to form the board.

country, providing only about 6 percent of the income of the average rural family. For their own use, rural families grow corn and vegetables on their plots and graze their cattle on communal land. Teenage boys herd flocks of sheep and goats high up in the mountains. Some relatively wealthy men in rural areas own cars or horses. The small Basotho ponies are famous for their ability to survive the cold and climb extremely steep paths.

Some rural Basotho run small trading stores, mostly selling food products, household items, and clothes, all manufactured in South Africa. Many rural families anxiously await the money sent from relatives working in South Africa,

Today, the best Basotho murals are created by farmworkers living in South Africa. These houses have several rooms, each with its own front door, for different members of the family. The slightly sloping roofs, made of metal sheets, cannot be seen from the front.

because then they can afford to buy supplies from these little stores.

Rural people live in various types of houses, many of which have walls made of earth. These walls are often beautifully decorated with engraved and painted patterns. Called *litema* (dee-tame-uh), this art tradition stretches back many hundreds of years. Today, the best *litema* is found on the houses of farmworkers living on the white-owned farms in South Africa.

Lesotho's larger towns, such as the capital of Maseru, have many of the features of similar-sized towns all over the world. There are government buildings, banks, luxury hotels, fast-food outlets, and many other stores that sell imported things. These centers are surrounded by sub-urban houses.▲

2

EARLY HISTORY

▼ MOSHOESHOE ▼

Moshoeshoe, son of a minor Bakoena chief, was born in Leribe (leh-ree-beh) in Lesotho in 1786. In about 1805 he underwent initiation. Initiation is a tough period of several weeks during which young men are isolated in a "bush school" and drilled in the practical skills, customs, history, and moral values of their people. Though he performed very well in the school, he was a rather strong-tempered young man, which caused his father and grandfather some concern. They took him to visit a relative called Mohlomi (moh-shlow-mee). Mohlomi was famous for his wisdom and the great wealth that he had built up by working as a doctor and healer and by creating numerous alliances. He was extremely well-traveled, knowledgeable, and curious about other peoples. He was a welcome visitor in many places in Southern Africa, and a host who was

always eager to receive visitors and news from distant places.

Mohlomi showed Moshoeshoe, who was called Letlama at this time, how great power and wealth could be achieved by promoting peace and good relations. Letlama decided to follow Mohlomi's example, but to get a good start, he needed cattle. After a successful cattle raid against a rival chief, Letlama adopted the name Moshoeshoe. This name imitates the "shweh-shweh" sound of a razor shaving. It celebrates the fact that Moshoeshoe had stripped his neighbor of his herd as easily as if he had been shaving off a beard.

By 1820, Moshoeshoe had several well-connected wives and a number of followers. He established himself as a minor chief, based on the flat-topped mountain of Botha-Bothe (boot-uh-boo-tay).

▼ THE TIME OF TROUBLES ▼

In the 1820s, a period of dreadful conflict and hardship in Southern Africa began, called the Lifaqane (Diffa-kwah-nee). Lifaqane means a "great scattering of people" or a "time of catastrophe" in Sotho languages.

The source of the tension was Zululand. Different chiefdoms were competing with each other for control of the region and the profitable trade with the whites on the coast.

The key figure among the competing chiefs was Shaka, king of the Zulu. He defeated most of the neighboring groups with his powerful army and new war tactics. Shaka ruled as a tyrant with an iron fist. Those who displeased him were often executed. When his beloved mother died, Shaka had many people killed so that the nation could share his sorrow, having suddenly lost their own loved ones.

This kind of government was very different from the more democratic traditions of Sotho-speakers. Basotho say, "A chief is a chief by the people,"

A Mosotho (singular of Basotho) warrior in the early 1800s carried a distinctive shield. A v-shaped brass collar was a medal of honor. This illustration was included in a book by Eugène Casalis about his experiences as a missionary among the Basotho.

meaning that a chief's power comes from the people and he must express their will.

From about 1820, people whom Shaka defeated and those who feared him, including his own outstanding generals, began to flee. Often they left hurriedly and in secret, taking little or no cattle or food. Many headed up the Drakensberg Mountains to the Highveld (hi-felt) plateau that lies high above the coast. The Highveld had suffered a bad drought and an epidemic of cattle disease. Food was scarce. The Sotho-speaking Highveld peoples could not feed the coastal refugees, who soon turned to raiding for food.

Raiding started a chain reaction: any people who lost their food and cattle to attackers were forced to become raiders themselves. To succeed, they employed the deadly military techniques that Shaka's refugees had brought to the Highveld. Soon, most of the interior of Southern Africa suffered great violence and starvation. Nobody was safe. Whole communities were wiped out by raiders. Others were scattered and absorbed into other armies of desperadoes. Many had to turn to cannibalism to survive.

Moshoeshoe was placed at risk by the powerful raiding armies that moved into his region and by the ambitions of his old enemies, the Tlokoa. In 1824, the Tlokoa besieged Moshoeshoe's mountain settlement of Botha-Bothe. Experts believe that Moshoeshoe arranged for the Zulu to attack the Tlokoa. This gave Moshoeshoe's people an opportunity to escape to another mountain that could be more easily defended. The new mountain was a two-day walk to the southwest, through territory occupied by cannibals.

On the way Moshoeshoe's grandfather was captured and devoured by cannibals. Years later, when peace returned, Moshoeshoe visited the cannibals and remarked that he would not punish them, because they were the living grave of his grandfather, and graves must be honored.

▼ THE FORMATION OF A NATION ▼

Moshoeshoe's new mountain was called Thaba-Bosiu, Mountain of the Night. Thaba-Bosiu (tub-uh-boss-you) is a natural fortress. It has very steep sides and only a few paths, which are easily defended by rolling boulders down on anyone who tries to come up. The flat top can accommodate thousands of people and cattle.

In these dangerous times, Moshoeshoe displayed great leadership. He played off his enemies against each other, so that they weakened each other. Meanwhile, exactly as Mohlomi had taught him, Moshoeshoe gained strength by promoting peace and attracting followers.

From far and wide people came to join Moshoeshoe's secure settlement. Anybody who came in peace was welcome. The population of

refugees from different cultures and backgrounds grew rapidly and learned the customs
of Moshoeshoe's people. For his followers,
Moshoeshoe adopted the name Basotho, a refer-
ence to the loincloths that his people wore. On
their mountain the young Basotho nation
formed an island of peace in a sea of unrest.

Moshoeshoe's love of peace (which he called
his "sister"), his diplomatic way of handling conflicts, and his emphasis on democratic government made him exceptional in Southern Africa
at that time. Although women were not officially
involved in decision-making about matters of
state, all Basotho men were expected to attend
the *pitso*, the court that gathered regularly to
debate important issues. In the *pitso* a man's
status was irrelevant; it was what he had to say
that counted. The humblest person could openly
criticize Moshoeshoe or any lesser chiefs. All
men were encouraged to develop the art of
poetic and persuasive argument, whether in matters of politics or philosophy. Fluency was, and
remains, greatly valued among Basotho.

▼ THE MISSIONARIES ▼

The first missionaries in the interior of South
Africa were stationed among a Tswana group
during the Lifaqane. When they felt their
community and mission were at risk from
aggressors, the missionaries sent for help. They

called on Khoekhoe people who had acquired guns and horses through contact with the Cape Colony. Armed with modern weapons, horsemen could move fast and easily fight off much larger armies that lacked these advantages.

Missionaries brought certain other advantages to African communities. They created trade and other links with the authorities at the Cape and introduced new foods and technologies. In violent times, the missionaries' message of peace, backed by the influence and guns to protect it, made them useful allies. Moshoeshoe was intrigued by this new combination of factors— missionaries, guns, and horses—and decided he wanted a missionary. He gave a frontier hunter a hundred cattle to "buy" him one.

In June 1833, three liberal missionaries from the Paris Evangelical Society were directed to Thaba-Bosiu by the hunter. They were led by Eugène Casalis (cuss-uh-lee). They had heard that Moshoeshoe would welcome them.

Moshoeshoe and Casalis quickly became friends. During the next twenty-three years, they spent many hours learning each other's philosophies, debating the meaning of life, and discussing how to ensure the survival of the nation. Casalis became an important spokesman for Moshoeshoe and the nation. He argued their case to Britain and other European powers.

Moshoeshoe was both fascinated by and supported many of the innovations brought by the

missionaries. He thought that writing was a wonderful thing: that one person's words could be relayed on paper to "speak" again at another place and time. He encouraged his sons and close relatives to acquire European education and accept Christianity, which he understood to be in harmony with most of Basotho philosophy and morality. He recognized that the Christian God was like the supreme God of the Basotho, called Molimo (maw-di-maw). Instead of humans communicating with God through the ancestors, Christians did so directly—something that Basotho never did with Molimo, because the supreme God was far too great. Moshoeshoe even allowed two of his wives to separate from him so that they could embrace Christianity, which does not recognize polygamy.

Moshoeshoe himself never publicly converted, because there was too much resistance to Christianity among his people. Many Basotho were outraged by the missionaries' arguments against key aspects of their society, including polygamy, *bohali*, and cattle raiding—which the missionaries saw as theft, rather than honorable. Most important was the missionaries' insistence that worship of the ancestors and all the customs connected with this were wrong. The customs included initiation schools for men and women; ceremonial singing, dancing, and drinking beer; and traditional medicine, divination, and rain-making. From the point of view of

This early drawing of the mission at Thaba-Bosiu shows the European buildings, including the house built for Moshoeshoe on top of the famous mountain. On the slopes and in the foreground are seen the original Basotho houses, built around cattle enclosures.

many Basotho, these customs were the key to being Basotho. Basotho saw no good reason to give them up or adopt other changes that the missionaries insisted on, such as Western clothes and rectangular houses laid out in straight rows.

▼ BATTLES FOR LAND ▼

One of the first political steps taken by Moshoeshoe through Casalis, in 1834, was to obtain official recognition of Lesotho by the British. He hoped the British would help protect his land against the Boers. Throughout his life Moshoeshoe tried to remain on good terms with the British and bring his nation under their protection. However, the British certainly did

not treat Basotho fairly. Between the 1830s and 1866, there were several major conflicts between the Boers and Basotho over land. Each time, the British intervened on the side of the Boers and gave them Basotho land. This led Moshoeshoe to remark, "You white people do not steal cattle, it's true, but you steal whole countries; and if you had your wish you would send us to pasture our cattle in the clouds."

By 1866 Moshoeshoe had been forced to sign away most of Lesotho's fertile land. He realized now that his nation would not survive against the Boers without British backing. He sent a famous appeal to the British saying he wanted the Basotho to be regarded as "the lice in the Queen's blanket," meaning that they would remain very close to Queen Victoria but rule themselves. The Queen probably did not like the comparison, but at a time when her empire seemed to be full of war, she probably appreciated loyal friends.

In 1868, Basotho were declared British subjects, and Lesotho finally came under British administration in 1869. Some of its fertile land was restored, but it had lost most of the farming land that it had once contained. For the Basotho, the acceptance of British officials over them and the loss of their best land were high prices to have paid for their survival, but they survived the colonial period in which many other African states were destroyed.▲

chapter

3

RELIGION AND CUSTOMS

▼ GENESIS ▼

In the Basotho genesis story, humans emerged from a cave deep within the earth. This cave is associated with a womb. The passage leading to the outside world is like the birth canal. At the place where humans reached the surface was a muddy bed of reeds. Humans had to emerge through the mud and reeds to reach daylight and begin life on Earth. This place is called Ntsoana Tsatsi (int-swun-nut-sut-see), which means "where the sun rises," or "where the light comes from."

Light, mud, and reeds were, and remain, important to Basotho beliefs in many ways. All are associated with the origins of life. Mud and reeds were the most important materials used in constructing the igloo-shaped Basotho houses that existed before the missionaries arrived. Like the

Basotho architecture has important symbolic meanings about creation. This relates both to the origin of the nation and to women's role in giving birth. Women are closely associated with the house and its materials and decorations.

cave in the story of origin, these houses were dark and it was necessary to exit down a low passage to the door. Houses faced east so that every morning there was light at the end of the tunnel, and people greeted the new day as if it were the very first day on earth at Ntsoana Tsatsi; as if each day was like being born again.

Basotho architecture thus has very important symbolic and religious meaning. Even today, when a child is born inside a house, it stays there for several days. A reed is placed in the doorway of the house, which is still often built of mud. Only when the child is carried past the reed to come outdoors into the light is it regarded as really being "born." This is like the nation

Litema decorations are named after the act of plowing fields. Some decorations look like plowed fields, others favor floral motifs. Farming was once women's work, but today Basotho farmworkers in the Free State are mostly men. These women are applying a red ocher border to their design.

passing through the mud and reeds at Ntsoana Tsatsi to come out into the light of the world. It is also as if the house stands for the mother's body—the house "gives birth to" the child.

Through ideas like this, women were, and to some extent still are, strongly associated with both the house and the earth in general. When a man's wife dies, it is said that "his house has fallen." Women also have a special relationship to the fertility of the earth and everything vegetable that grows on it, including reeds. While women's lives and work once centered on the household and farming, men were concerned with the cattle and their corral, or *kraal*. Today, of course, very few families continue to live according to this traditional pattern, because work has changed.

Ntsoana Tsatsi is a place in the Free State, near the town of Vrede. Excavations there have revealed traces of a settlement, dating to 1500 AD, that belonged to the early Bakoena people who later became Basotho.

▼ THE ANCESTORS ▼

The ancestors were people's main link with the spiritual world. For many Basotho today this is still true, even if they are Christian. Ancestors are the messengers, or mediators, between humans and Molimo, the Supreme Being.

When a family member dies, he or she joins the ancestors, called *balimo* or *badimo*. In the past, senior women were buried in the court-yard, or *lapa*, of their home. Men were buried at the cattle *kraal*. Nowadays the dead are often buried far away, but ancestors remain a very important part of the family. Even Christian Basotho point out that the Bible instructs every-one to love and respect their parents; it does not say this must stop when they die.

The ancestors are regarded as ever-present, but their presence is felt more strongly on some occasions than others. Whenever an animal sacrifice is made at a ceremony, the ancestors gather around, because blood is their special substance. Apart from breath, which is hard to

During women's initiation, many comparisons are drawn between women and the house. These graduates (above) wear red earth and carry mats of reeds—both are materials used in architecture and linked to the idea of fertility. Balloons on some mats (below) symbolize the breath and spirit of life and pregnancy. They are a modern replacement for the inflated bladders of sacrificed animals.

capture, blood is most closely associated with human and animal life and is where the human spirit is located. In some ways, blood is like rain—a liquid without which there would be no life. When sacrificial blood falls on the earth, it links life and the living with the earth where the ancestors live and where food grows. Red earth, or ocher, is called *letsoku*, "the blood of the earth" and is especially treasured. In the past it was important in rain-making ceremonies. Today it still has religious use in mural art and initiation ceremonies, which all promote the idea of fertility.

Basotho ideas about sacrifice influenced their acceptance of Christianity. Animal sacrifice was used in the Old Testament as a way of communicating with God. In the New Testament, Christ gives up his own life to save others. Drinking communion wine at Christian religious ceremonies is a symbol of drinking the blood of Christ. These factors together make Easter far more important than Christmas for many African Christians, because Easter celebrates the time of Christ's self-sacrifice.

Today, few Basotho, whether in the rural areas or the towns, forget their ancestors. Every important family occasion involves some ceremony that addresses the ancestors. Even many Basotho Christian ministers address the ancestors and honor their graves.

In early Basotho houses, the most sacred part of the house was a raised platform opposite the door. Here were kept pots for food and water. These were closely associated with the ancestors, because a Mosotho should think of them at every meal. By the 1930s, these platforms were a focus of decoration (left). Today they have become mud racks that blend tradition with Christian symbols. The example below was made by Emily Shabalala.

▼ DIVINERS ▼

In the past, Basotho had two main kinds of doctors. Herbalists specialized in physical complaints and provided natural medicines. Diviners (*linohe*) dealt with spiritual matters, communicating directly with the ancestors and using divination objects to read their messages.

A new kind of spiritual healing, which directly accesses the ancestors' healing power through trances and visions, spread from the Zulu people on the coast to Lesotho in the late 1800s. This kind of healer is called *lethuela* (let-way-la) or, in Zulu, *sangoma* (sang-gaw-ma).

Mathuela (plural of *lethuela*) and other traditional doctors use their skills to heal the body by focusing on body, mind, and spirit all at once, combining the Western professions of doctor, psychologist, and spiritual adviser.

Many *mathuela* are also members of African Christian sects that harmonize African religion with Christianity. Among Basotho, the most important sect is the Apostolic Church, which has many branches in the region. Apostolics pray to God and the ancestors, and *mathuela* call on both these forces to heal patients' troubles or to pray for peace, rain, and plenty. During the violent time before South Africa became a democratic country in 1994, many believed that all the bloodshed had soiled the earth and offended the ancestors. As a result, the ancestors

Caves in Southern Africa have been used in worship for thousands of years. The ancient cave paintings of the San people record trance sessions and religious visions. Today, many Basotho use caves for healing and other religious ceremonies. Here (left), a priestess of the Apostolic Church, which blends Christianity with traditional ancestor worship, calls on God and the ancestors to help heal a patient. This enormous cave in the Free State, called Saltpeterskranz, has a wide reputation as a place of extraordinary spiritual power. It draws pilgrims and trainee *mathuela*, diviners, from thousands of miles away. Often people take holy water and earth home with them.

At Modderpoort in the Free State are San caves, an Anglican mission, and a holy cave, where a famous Basotho prophet and healer once lived. She sealed the tiny cave by walling it up with earth. Today it is a chapel. After prayers in the chapel, this Apostolic priestess (right) baptized a mental patient at a stream in the valley far below. The ceremony included prayers to God and the ancestors, Bible readings chosen by opening the Bible at random places, and offerings placed on the ground and in the water. Healing mud and other medicines were also collected. Modderpoort is the birthplace of Nobel Prize winner Archbishop Desmond Tutu.

withheld the rain, resulting in a terrible drought.

The focus on earth in Basotho religion makes caves, rivers, and other natural places important sites of worship and healing. The earth is nature's drugstore where all the herbs needed for medicine grow. Rivers are important places for women's initiation and for healing baptisms that combine Basotho and Christian beliefs.

Caves are like Ntsoana Tsatsi, the Basotho birthplace. For thousands of years caves were used for religious ceremonies by the San people (once called "Bushmen"), who were the first inhabitants of this region. The San influenced many aspects of Basotho belief and culture. Today, religious ceremonies continue in these caves. Basotho paint on the walls of caves like the San, who created beautiful rock art of magical humans and animals. Often, *mathuela* lead patients in circular dances at important places of worship. These healing dances are called *hlophe* (shlo-peh).

Most *mathuela* go through periods of training while living with another *lethuela* to learn the use of medicines and how to improve spiritual communication. Training may last a few weeks or even years. A person enters training because of troubling dreams or illnesses, which indicate that the ancestors want the person to train. ▲

A Diviner's Graduation

A cow is sacrificed at the graduation of a *lethuela*. It is killed to ask *badimo* to stop the initiate's ailments. *Badimo* are asked to guide the new *lethuela* to be a great healer.

The graduate sucks at the animal's windpipe to gain strength and inspiration, and everyone eats the meat. Some blood soaks into the earth to feed the ancestors. Sorghum beer is brewed in honor of the ancestors, and fermenting grain is thrown onto the earth to ask them for fertility and abundance.

Diviners from the whole region usually attend the night-long event, dressed in their finest ceremonial clothes. It is an extremely impressive and spiritually powerful event. The diviners (below) frequently halt their circular dances to pray to the ancestors in the earth. Many diviners and other guests go into trances during the night of dancing and singing. Trancing affects people differently. Some become mediums who speak with the voice of the spirit that has possessed them. Others lose consciousness and their bodies jerk and dance uncontrollably while the spirit possesses them.

A group of diviners address their prayers to the ancestors in the earth.

chapter

4

THE ARTS

MANY OF THE TRADITIONAL ARTS OF THE Basotho are connected to religion. At important ceremonies, many art forms occur at the same time.

▼ MUSIC ▼

Music calls the ancestors, and songs are heard by them. *Mathuela* beat the *sekupu* drum to establish a link to the ancestors. Sometimes *mathuela* dance to become possessed.

Basotho have several string instruments, mostly consisting of a single string attached to a stick or reed. These may have been adopted from the San people. Also used are body and ankle rattles made of pebble-filled leather pouches, rattling belts made from metal bottle tops, and strands of bells, usually worn by diviners.

Basotho have a rich selection of traditional

DANCE

Dance plays an important role in spiritual possession, but it is also used for entertainment and expressing unity.

The *litolobonya* dance is performed and attended only by women who have had at least one child. Another important dance performed by women wearing matching costumes is the *mokhibo*, a dance of national celebration.

Men also have special dances. Migrant men performed these dances and invented others on the mines, where the divisions between ethnic groups were encouraged by the mining companies.

These young women are demonstrating an entertaining dance that features paper skirts.

songs. Men's war songs, *mokorotlo*, keep up men's spirits in difficult times, such as initiation, and are also used for prayer and celebrations. Men used *mangae* songs to cry out to their ancestors during initiation, but today both men and women use *mangae* to express their deepest feelings. Many other songs, *lipina*, are sung by women during initiation or for entertainment. Such traditions formed the basis for new, urban music that was developed by Basotho migrants and is very popular among Basotho today. Today, Basotho are also fans of contemporary music from the rest of the world.

▼ LITERATURE ▼

Oral literature includes songs and heroic praises, *lithoko* (dee-talk-o), which are half way between speaking and singing. *Lithoko*, taught during men's initiation, teach the history of heroic ancestors and the Basotho values that made them great. Initiates also compose praise poems about themselves, announcing who they are. This teaches them poetic fluency and defines them in terms of Basotho culture. The man on the cover of this book is singing his praise song at his graduation ceremony.

Basotho quickly became literate through the influence of the missionaries and their own interest. Today, there are many Basotho authors writing in Sesotho and English. Scholarly works

by Basotho academics form an important part of Basotho literature today.

▼ VISUAL ARTS ▼

Today, the most important visual arts among Basotho are mural painting (*litema*) and dress. Many traditions, such as pottery and basketry, have been largely replaced by Western items, but the distinctive Basotho hat, woven from grass, is still popular with Basotho and tourists alike.

The centuries-old mural tradition has developed wonderful new designs and is now much more colorful than in the past. Most designs are still inspired by plants and flowers, which are symbols of natural fertility. Today these are often combined with Christian elements. Although many bright colors are now used, earth ochres and the symbolic colors of black, white, and red are still very important. During the struggle against apartheid in South Africa, some women painted their houses in the colors of the African National Congress to show their support for this political party that later headed South Africa's first democratic government.

The Basotho are famous for the colorful blankets they wear. After white traders established themselves in Lesotho, the design of many blankets was based on the murals on houses. The blankets now form part of Basotho traditional

Floral motifs on houses in the Free State are often bold and beautiful. The design over the doorway above features a cutout flower; the one below uses traditional colors on a side wall.

Beadwork is an important Basotho art form. This diviner has created beaded designs inspired by the ancestors during dreams.

dress. The use of beadwork and body painting is still common today.

Like all other southern African peoples, Basotho are thoroughly involved in all aspects of contemporary life, and often their activities are not much affected by their ethnic upbringing. This is also true of Basotho artists, who are part of the arts scene in Lesotho, South Africa, and other places. ▲

chapter

5

COLONIALISM AND APARTHEID

▼ COLONIALISM ▼

Moshoeshoe died in March 1870. In the same year, Britain began its direct rule of Basutoland. Direct rule meant that magistrates introduced laws to promote the Christian, Western way of life, undermine the power of Basotho chiefs, and discourage customs like polygamy, *bohali*, and initiation. In 1871, the British economized by placing Basutoland under the Cape Colony, which was itself granted self-government by the British in 1872. Basutoland was then ruled by the Cape.

In 1870, an event of great significance for the whole of Southern Africa occurred. Rich diamond deposits were discovered at Kimberley. The mine soon became the largest man-made hole in the world.

Mining required labor. Black men from all

Basotho miners have played an important role in the economy of Southern Africa for more than a century. These men are members of a Basotho dance group from a gold mine near Johannesburg.

over Southern Africa were hired at low wages by companies that made enormous profits from their labor. Miners were soon housed in compounds designed like concentration camps. They were subjected to humiliating body searches to prevent them from stealing diamonds.

Diamond mining introduced the system of migrant labor. The discovery of gold in Johannesburg in 1885 extended it. The corporation that controlled diamond mining soon dominated gold mining too. During the next century, the same corporation, the Anglo American Corporation, controlled many of the big companies of South Africa, which grew wealthy through exploiting workers by paying low wages.

The 1870s were very prosperous for Lesotho. To supply the Kimberley miners, food production was stepped up by using ploughs that were pulled by oxen and driven by men (instead of the traditional agriculture of women using hoes). Many Basotho leased land owned by Boer cattle farmers, and grew superior grain for sale. Basotho men and women migrated to Kimberley and other towns and to white-owned farms. There they earned wages or sold items and services in demand. Many wanted cash to buy guns, cattle, horses, and blankets. Trading stores sprang up in Lesotho where traders offered Western goods for cash or traded them for commodities like wool.

With these economic changes, Basotho, along with the rest of Southern Africa, entered the modern era.

▼ WARS ▼

The British and the Cape Colony hoped to unite the two British colonies of the Cape and Natal with the two Boer republics of the Transvaal and the Orange Free State to form the Union of South Africa. Boers would consider this only if African societies had no access to guns, so the British tried to disarm all Africans.

The Basotho refused to give up their guns. A rebellion, called the Gun War, broke out in Basutoland (1880–81). The Cape government

spent so many millions of dollars trying to crush Basotho resistance that the Cape government fell, the idea of a union collapsed, and the Cape asked Britain to take back control of Basutoland. Basotho became the only black people in South Africa who kept the guns they had worked so hard for.

British authority thus returned to Basotholand in 1884, but with a new policy of indirect rule. This meant that the British used the chiefs as tools for getting what they wanted, instead of undermining the chiefs as they had done before.

The Gun War was a victory for Basotho, but there were many new problems in Basotho society. First, Moshoeshoe's sons fought among themselves and often opposed Letsie, Moshoeshoe's heir. Second, the introduction of a Western economy had changed the power of chiefs. Commoners who had become wealthy through farming or trading could now run their own lives. Under British indirect rule many chiefs became corrupt. They lost the respect of ordinary people, who began to believe that the best plan for the future was to abandon tradition and follow the route of Western education and Christianity. Finally, Lesotho quickly became overpopulated, overgrazed, and too intensively farmed, leading to land shortages and bad erosion. More and more Basotho chose to farm as tenants on the white farms in the Free State.

They were so successful there that the Boers soon began to demand laws to suppress them.

In the mid-1890s a cattle epidemic wiped out much of Lesotho's wealth. But war finally broke out between the British and the Boers over control of the gold mines in the Transvaal. The Basotho regained their losses by supplying grain and horses to both sides during the Anglo-Boer War (1899–1902). Most Basotho hoped that the British would win the war, return land to Lesotho, and protect the rights of Africans that Boers denied. The British did win, but once again it was more important to them to keep the Boers happy than to pay attention to the hopes and concerns of Africans. In fact, from the formation of the Union of South Africa in 1910, through the apartheid era that began in 1948, and until South Africa became a democratic, nonracist country in 1994, Lesotho either lived in fear of being incorporated into South Africa or it suffered oppression in Lesotho that was linked to the situation in South Africa.

▼ THE TWENTIETH CENTURY ▼

Moshoeshoe's great-grandson, Letsie II, joined other Basotho chiefs and educated elites in forming the African Native National Congress in 1912. Later renamed the African National Congress (ANC), this is the party that finally led South Africa to democracy. For half a century,

The twentieth century brought many changes in Basotho life. The relationship between tradition and modernization was hotly debated. These photographs (above and opposite page) from the 1930s show headgear that is no longer worn today.

the ANC tried peaceful ways to achieve equal rights for blacks. However, it was outlawed, its leaders like Nelson Mandela were imprisoned in 1963, and the ANC was forced to consider itself at war with the racist South African government. Some Basotho played leading roles in starting South Africa's first trade union. In later years, unions became an important way of fighting for fair labor conditions in South Africa.

Between the two World Wars, in which thousands of Basotho soldiers fought as loyal British soldiers, tensions in Lesotho between chiefs and commoners increased. The chiefs and British authorities cooperated with each other, and they had two main critics. The first was the

Today, Lesotho has the highest literacy rate in Africa, and Basotho maintain many of their traditions. This feather headdress is similar to the ostrich feathers worn by the men on page 50.

Christian-educated elite of the Basotho Progressive Association (BPA), which was in favor of modernization and abolishing chiefly privileges. The second was the Commoners League. The League believed that Basotho should return to their traditions, restore the proper caring relationship between chiefs and commoners, and reject white culture and government. They agreed with the Africanist message of African American Marcus Garvey, who proclaimed, "Africa for the Africans." This political view is known as Pan Africanism.

Britain realized that Lesotho needed democratic reform to prevent another rebellion. Reforms began to reduce, limit, and control the

power of chiefs, and commoners were given more representation in government. The power of the king was reduced, and he became increasingly answerable to a National Council.

In 1952, Ntsu Mokhehle formed the Basutoland Congress Party (BCP) to demand an independent democracy for Lesotho. The BCP combined the modernizing ideas of the BPA elite with the Africanist position of the Commoners League. It was linked both to the ANC in South Africa and to Pan Africanists in South Africa and other parts of Africa, such as Kwame Nkrumah who led Ghana to independence from Britain. From the 1950s onward, Africans throughout Africa, who were fighting to regain power over their colonized countries, were influenced by socialist ideas that emphasized human equality and criticized economic exploitation.

Religion played an important role in political developments in Lesotho. The Protestant Church established by Casalis supported the democratic demands of commoners, while the Catholic Church largely supported the chiefs. In later years this difference sharpened.

In 1957, two new political parties were formed. The first was the royalist Marematlou Party (MTP), formed by chiefs who wanted the king, Moshoeshoe II, to have real political power and not just be a figurehead in a democratic country. The second party was the Basutoland

National Party (BNP) which wanted to co-operate with apartheid South Africa and prevent friction with this powerful neighbor. Strongly supported by the Catholic Church, South Africa, and West Germany, the BNP also wanted to preserve chiefly power and combat democratization and socialism.

▼ ELECTIONS IN LESOTHO ▼

The BCP won the first elections in Lesotho in 1960, but Lesotho did not yet have a democratic constitution or government. Chiefs were still appointed into government. Chiefs had enough power to prevent the goals of the BCP, which became hostile and radical. Many of its rural supporters were frightened away. At this time many Basotho in the rural areas had little understanding of voting or how Lesotho's move toward independence was linked to other struggles throughout Africa. The BCP did little to correct this and get its message across, so the BNP won the 1965 elections. Women had been excluded from the elections, and only about 10 percent of adults had voted.

Between the 1960 and 1965 elections, Lesotho drew up a constitution for independence. It was based on the British system, in which the king is a figurehead and the senate or upper house consists of nobles or people appointed by the king. Most power lies with the

Many Basotho blankets have floral designs (top left). Designs often incorporate other symbols, such as corn for fertility (top right), and national symbols such as the Basotho hat (middle). The close relationship between Britain and Basotho is shown by images of the British crown and items from World War II (middle right, bottom left).

elected representatives in the lower house of commoners. Most Basotho were happy with this constitution, except the royalists and King Moshoeshoe II.

▼ INDEPENDENCE ▼

After independence in 1966, the BNP government, led by Chief Leabua Jonathan, had difficulties ruling, because the educated Basotho who ran government departments were mainly BCP supporters. The BNP forced most of them to leave and hired many South African advisers, which created resentment in Lesotho.

By the time of the next elections in 1970, the BNP had achieved little, while the BCP had carefully built its support throughout the country. The BCP easily won the next election in 1970, but the BNP refused to hand over power. It declared a State of Emergency, suspended the constitution, threw hundreds of BCP supporters into jail, used the army and police to crush all opposition, and assassinated its enemies. Many felt that South Africa was behind these undemocratic tactics. At first, Britain and other countries suspended aid to Lesotho in protest. However, Lesotho suffered a terrible drought and British and other international aid poured back into the country. This reduced both the BNP's reliance on South Africa and the pressure on the BNP to restore democracy.

As South Africa became more repressive and internationally unpopular and resistance inside South Africa stepped up, Leabua Jonathan reversed his friendly attitude to South Africa. He became critical of South Africa, supportive of the ANC, and forged links with the communist countries of USSR, China, Cuba, and North Korea. He wanted to turn Lesotho into a socialist one-party state under his dictatorship.

Meanwhile, the BCP still hoped to regain control of the government that it had been legally elected to run. It organized the Lesotho Liberation Army (LLA), with support from Libya and the Pan African Congress. Strangely enough, South Africa was now prepared to support the BCP—which it had once opposed—in order to destroy the dictatorship of Leabua Jonathan that South Africa had helped create. Everyone had changed sides.

In 1986, a military coup encouraged by South Africa overthrew Leabua Jonathan, but the corruption and violence continued in Lesotho. Finally, in March 1993, the military government fulfilled its promise to hold a democratic election. Over 70 percent of the voters voted. The BCP won more than 75 percent of the votes. After being denied the right to rule that it had won twenty-three years earlier, the BCP now controls Lesotho.▲

Glossary

bohali A payment of cattle to the bride's family.

commoners Those who do not have noble rank.

coup Takeover of a government, often violent.

desperados Violent bandits.

dictatorship Rule by one person or a small group, generally oppressive.

elites Those who have power as a result of education or rank.

epidemic A disease that affects much of a population.

Highveld A high plateau in Southern Africa.

landlocked Having no access to the sea.

one-party state A state in which only one political party is allowed.

polygamy Having more than one spouse.

socialist A social system not based solely on private ownership.

tenant farmer One who farms on leased land.

tenant laborer A laborer who lives and works on a farm owned by someone else.

trekked Traveled by ox wagon.

tyrant A brutal dictator, often a ruler who has illegally taken control.

For Further Reading

Calinicos, Lulu. *Gold and Workers, 1886–1924.* Johannesburg: Raven, 1985.

Gill, Stephen. *A Short History of Lesotho.* Morija, Lesotho: Morija Museum and Archives, 1995.

Omer-Cooper, J.D. *History of Southern Africa.* Portsmouth, N.H.: Heinemann, 1994.

Challenging Reading

Ashton, Hugh. *The Basuto.* London: Oxford Univ. Press, 1952.

Casalis, Eugène. *The Basutos.* Morija, Lesotho: Morija Museum and Archives, n.d.

Haliburton, Gordon. *Historical Dictionary of Lesotho.* Metuchen, N.J.: Scarecrow Press, 1977.

Lye, William F., and Murray, Colin. *Transformations on the Highveld: The Tswana and Southern Sotho.* Cape Town: David Philip, 1980.

Orpen, Joseph. *History of the Basutos of South Africa.* Mazenod, Lesotho: Mazenod Book Centre, 1979.

Setiloane, Gabriel. *The Image of God Among the Sotho-Tswana.* Rotterdam: Balkema, 1976.

Thompson, Leonard. *Survival in Two Worlds: Moshoeshoe of Lesotho 1786–1870.* Oxford: Clarendon Press, 1975.

Index

ABOUT THE AUTHOR

Born in Zimbabwe, Gary van Wyk holds graduate degrees in law and fine arts and a Ph.D. in Art History and Archaeology from Columbia University, New York, where he was a Fulbright Scholar. His dissertation research on the Basotho received the Rockefeller Foundation's African Dissertation Award. His art and photography have been exhibited and published internationally. He is engaged in a range of scholarly, educational, and museum projects on African culture and is preparing a volume on the Basotho for Harry N. Abrams Publishers, New York. He is currently Editor of Special Projects at The Rosen Publishing Group and consulting editor for the Heritage Library of African Peoples.

PHOTO CREDITS

All photos by Gary van Wyk, except p. 24 courtesy of Morija Museum and Archives, Lesotho; pp. 38 top, 54, 55 © McGregor Museum, Kimberley, South Africa; p. 58 Frasers Trading Co. (Pty.) Ltd.

LAYOUT AND DESIGN

Kim Sonsky